Making ADHD Make Sense

Making ADHD Make Sense

A Guided Journal

Alex Partridge

sheldon PRESS

First published by Sheldon Press in 2025
An imprint of John Murray Press

1

Copyright © Alex Partridge 2025

A CIP catalogue record for this title is available from the British Library

Hardback ISBN 978 1 399 82781 2
ebook ISBN 978 1 399 82782 9

Typeset by KnowledgeWorks Global Ltd.

Printed and bound in the United States of America

John Murray Press policy is to use papers that are natural, renewable and recyclable products and made from wood grown in sustainable forests. The logging and manufacturing processes are expected to conform to the environmental regulations of the country of origin.

John Murray Press
Carmelite House
50 Victoria Embankment
London EC4Y 0DZ

www.sheldonpress.co.uk

John Murray Press, part of Hodder & Stoughton Limited
An Hachette UK company

The authorized representative in the EEA is Hachette Ireland, 8 Castlecourt Centre, Dublin 15, D15 XTP3, Ireland (email: info@hbgi.ie)

Contents

Introduction

It's been six months since my first book, entitled *Now It All Makes Sense*, was published. Seeing it in people's hands and in bookshops all around the world creates a surreal feeling within me that I'll never, ever get bored of.

My aim with the book was simple: to provide a toolkit for people with ADHD to use to steer them on to a path of self-understanding. Too many people, particularly women and girls, have been let down for too long, walking on the wrong path, a confusing path where being told they're 'too much' or 'too sensitive' is common; a path where little made sense, with no understanding of why the tiniest real or perceived criticism created an instant intense physical pain, why others appear to glide through life with ease, yet certain things for them are incredibly challenging, why their brain constantly felt like it was inhabited by ten highly caffeinated squirrels, and why being exhausted is their natural state of being.

I desperately wanted the book to shine a light on the fact that many of these confusions could be explained by undiagnosed ADHD; it's a beautiful moment when someone experiences this realisation and suddenly their whole life makes sense. They were never broken, they were simply different, and they were always enough.

It's been truly heart-warming to read the many positive reviews from people who say the book guided them to that moment.

Why I journal

As I went through the same eye-opening process myself, when I got my ADHD diagnosis aged 34, I quickly discovered the importance of journalling. It was, and still very much is, the key to me successfully managing the more challenging aspects of ADHD.

One of those aspects is the phenomenon known as 'object permanence'. This describes the idea that when something leaves your line of sight it leaves your mind, and ceases to exist. It explains why so many of us forget basic things such as reusable shopping bags or emptying the washing machine. It also applies to thoughts. I can hyper-focus on a thought but if I don't write it down, my mind will move on to the next thought and the previous thought will cease to exist.

This is where the journal is vital.

In *Now It All Makes Sense,* I explain how I don't believe ADHD to be a deficit of attention but instead a deficit of self-awareness. After all, we've spent a lifetime masking, playing a character called 'normal', so we don't fully understand who we truly are. The journal helps by reminding me of the questions I need to ask myself, and by providing a clear place for me to write down my answers. Over time, this simple exercise allows me to build up my self-awareness, which enables me to better assess if something (or someone!) is a good fit for me. Without self-awareness, an ADHD person will continue to act on short-term dopamine spikes, they will say 'yes' to that new relationship, new job or new hobby, only to abandon it after a short while because it's not a good fit with who they truly are.

To bolster my understanding of my inner self, I intentionally notice my knee-jerk reactions. A knee-jerk reaction is a reaction to an external stimulus that your body creates from your subconscious, and it is not affected by the masked version of you. These reactions are totally raw and offer a window into your core values, and a path to your inner child. For example, imagine you're browsing a newspaper, you spot an advertisement for a musical theatre audition and, before you have time to process the moment, you instantly fill with excitement – but then you remember that your parents want you to be a doctor, so you push down your excitement and ignore the musical theatre advert. I use the journal to write down knee-jerk reactions like that and, over time, it enables me to create a clear picture and to see my true passions.

When someone with ADHD truly understands who they are, they stop saying 'yes' to things that don't align with their core values. When this happens, they notice fewer things get abandoned, which in turn boosts their mood, lowers shame and massively increases their self-confidence.

It is so important for ADHDers to remind themselves of their core values, beliefs and motivations. As Dr Ned Hallowell explained perfectly on the ADHD Chatter podcast, people with ADHD have a peculiar perception of time; they either live in the 'now' or the 'not now'. We can fixate on things, ideas or people, but unless we journal those moments, the feelings associated with them will float off out of our memory. This is particularly important for ADHD entrepreneurs, or anyone wanting to stick at a hobby or a new relationship. If we don't journal the feelings of excitement that triggered our desire to start the 'thing', we will lose sight of it, it will leave our consciousness and we will forget why we started the business, fell in love or bought that domain.

Journalling also helps me combat the effects of imposter syndrome because, as Ned Hallowell implies above, object permanence also applies to memories. For example, when I complete a challenging task like speaking on stage (or writing a book!), unless I journal the memory, it fades into nothingness and I forget that I'm capable of doing that task. So when the opportunity comes to do the same task again, I feel like an imposter, a fraud - like they've asked the wrong person.

I use my journal to keep those memories front and centre, so when I sit down to write a new book or before I walk on stage to give a talk, I can read my memory in my journal. This habit immediately reminds me that I am the right person for the job.

Another useful purpose of my journal is to challenge my inner critic when RSD (Rejection Sensitive Dysphoria) strikes. The opposite of RSD is a euphoric response to praise, so it's useful to have a list of my positive traits and achievements available to read in moments when I'm feeling triggered. It won't completely erase the nasty effects of RSD but it will help to balance my emotions when I'm faced with a real or a perceived criticism.

ADHD comes with an abundance of energy, creativity and fun, but with great energy comes great crashes. It's essential to be aware of when your energy is running low and when you need to take a break. We all have unique indicators of burnout - our body will give us signals that it's time to pause and rest. However, as life with ADHD can be fast-paced, it's easy to ignore these early warning signs. I journal as a mechanism to write down my early warning signs of fatigue so that I can take action and divert my path before I encounter a full-blown episode of burnout. My early warning signs are an increase in irritability, eating rubbish food and neglecting my exercise routine.

After my ADHD diagnosis, I went through a grieving process for the life I could have lived if I had lived a life truer to myself. I still reflect and get sad at how much I masked, shape-shifted and put other people's needs before my own. However, the mask was very firmly in place, and simply receiving an ADHD diagnosis didn't make it come off straight away. I use my journal to write down my daily behaviour, how I respond in different social interactions, and if my responses to demands on my time aligned with my own wants and needs. Saying 'yes' to things I didn't really want to do was so ingrained that it's almost impossible to stop it overnight, but my journal helps me track my progress and adjust accordingly. Adapting from a 'yes' man to a 'can I let you know tomorrow?' man takes practice, and a journal is a great judgement-free accountability buddy.

Additionally, romantic relationships require a lot of attention and benefit greatly from the use of a journal. As time goes past, things will happen during the course of your relationship that bring you closer together, and things will happen that create friction. In these moments, it's important to write down the cause and effect of each event and use this as a reminder when you, as a couple, sit down and communicate how you're feeling. Time can move quickly, and positive and negative moments can soon be forgotten, but the feeling associated with them can remain and, if not addressed and communicated, they can compound either negatively or positively, often resulting in an unannounced outburst that neither of you saw coming. Journalling enables me to keep note of those moments and communicate my feelings, avoiding the silent build-up of resentment and a resulting argument.

Penultimately, my journal allows me to avoid the ADHD tax. In *Now It All Makes Sense*, I detail the 'boom and bust' cycle and explain how many people with ADHD can spend a lot of money on a new hobby (the boom) but then lose interest (the bust). Not only is this expensive, but it also creates shame because we have a tendency to proclaim our new hobby to everyone around us, only to feel embarrassed as we abandon that same hobby. In those 'boom' moments, it's important to pause and reflect on whether or not this new hobby is truly a good fit for you. The journal provides a tool to write down the qualities of the new hobby which you can use to see if they're aligned with your personal qualities. As an additional bonus, the time it takes to do this exercise is often sufficient for you to pass through the 'boom' phase without having spent any money on yet another website domain!

Finally, my journal allows me to stay sober. When I chatted to Dr James Kustow, a leading ADHD specialist, he remarked on the fact that many people with ADHD struggle to stay clean from their addictions because they forget about the reason they stopped. In other words, they lose the connection to the intense feeling of despair that motivated them to stop in the first place. My journal, as well as sobriety support groups, is a critical tool that allows me to keep the connection with that memory, which serves as a daily reminder of my 'why' reason for staying sober.

In summary, my journal is an extremely useful tool that allows me to get thoughts out of my head and down on to paper. My head is a chaotic place with multiple thoughts happening simultaneously, each one pulling me in a different direction, most of them not worthy of any attention. Without a journal, the thoughts have no filter, no method to separate the useful from the not useful, so the chaos turns into overwhelm, anxiety and decision paralysis. A journal allows me to extract the useful thoughts, organise them and turn them into an action that furthers my life in the direction that I want it to go in.

How to use this journal

This journal is designed to be, just like you, a work in progress. It can be picked up or put down whenever you like. I prefer to add to my journal daily but sometimes life gets busy and I only manage to add to it two or three times a week. I find it useful to keep my journal near me at all times in case something happens that I want to write down. Otherwise, if I leave my journal at home, I often forget about the thing I want to write down!

Either way, it's a judgement-free zone and should not be paired with any form of pressure.

The book is split into two key parts – a guided journal section, followed by journalling pages. The guided journal is laid out in a similar order as my main book, working through key areas that many people with ADHD find challenging. Each chapter of the guided journal has several sections; you can do one section a day if that's all you have time for, or more if you would like. You don't have to work through chapter by chapter, but it might be easier to keep your place if you miss a few days, if you do. Each new daily section starts with a prompt allowing you to reflect on your state of mind that day, and each chapter ends with a chance for you to review where you are, or your 'progress', if you prefer.

At the end of the guided journal, you will find more traditional journal pages inviting you to start a regular habit, and to continue tracking all your achievements – the small wins and the big successes.

It's useful to find a quiet space where you can hyper-focus on your own thoughts without any external distractions. You can, of course, share your

xii Making ADHD Make Sense

journal entries with your partner, a friend or a family member, or even body double with someone and journal together.

It's also important to remember that there are no right or wrong journal entries. Whatever comes into your mind in the moment is perfect. Also, as with anything, you change and grow as a person, so you might read a journal entry from the past and not recognise yourself, that's completely normal and is an indicator that you've grown, you've moved closer to living a life true to yourself, and that should be applauded.

And always remember, whatever stage of your ADHD journey you're at, you have never been broken, just different, and you have always been enough!

1

Feeling Different

Today I am …

....

....

Feeling different

For as long as I can remember, I've had a suspicion that I am unusual. As a child I found myself often doing the following:

- copying others' mannerisms and their tone of voice
- pretending to share their interests and hobbies
- altering who I was in order to appear likeable.

Hating confrontation, I often said 'yes' to things I didn't want to do. I'd be filled with an initial excitement for something that would make me impulsively say 'yes!' and would then be trapped in that situation as I didn't know how to have the conversation required for me to leave.

Our differences run deep and many of us are aware of them from our earliest childhood days. For example, many of us experience emotions more profoundly than everyone else, even if we don't always show them. They can overwhelm us out of nowhere, caused by things as trivial as getting new shoes, or waiting for a favourite TV show to start.

We are highly sensitive to perceived injustice, and from our earliest days, situations that we feel are unfair or carry undeserved criticism can feel like a silent explosion inside us.

You may carry these incidents, occasions and childhood encounters deep inside you, and the emotions they cause still sit within, often exploding out of nowhere. Perhaps you are hyperfocused on a particular memory and suddenly feel an urge to burst into tears, or you become fixated on a specific injustice and feel overwhelmed by anger.

Before we go further, let's take a moment for you to reflect on some of the experiences from your past that made you feel different. On the next page, make a note of five occasions when your 'difference' felt most pronounced – and spend a moment thinking about how those events make you feel now.

1. ....

....

....

....

2. ....

....

....

....

3. ....

....

....

....

4. ....

....

....

....

5. ....

....

....

....

Today I am …

....

....

Let's look further at your differences.

If you have ADHD, you are probably aware that some of your everyday differences are almost superpowers. Like many superpowers, they are far from unproblematic, each of them with pros and cons, making life more of a challenge than it would otherwise be. For example:

I have heightened intuition. I have always been able to 'read' people exceptionally well.

Pro: I can tell when someone's not being genuine. I hear the tiny fluctuations in their tone of voice. I'm a human lie detector.

Con: It is also a curse: walking into a busy room and picking up on negative energy towards you.

My ADHD makes me a great driver.

Pro: I can hyperfocus on the road. I'm super-fixated and aware of everything around me. My hyper-vigilance means I know exactly what's happening half a mile in front of me and I know what's happening half a mile behind me.

I can react superfast when another driver does something stupid.

Con: I get lost easily, so I'm totally dependent on Google Maps. And I get really, really upset in traffic.

Think about your two greatest daily superpowers. What are their pros and cons?

1.   Pros   2.   Pros

     Cons   Cons

Your family and your friends

Those of us with ADHD live in a constant state of 'now'. It's why we often struggle to maintain friendships and why our family members become so inpatient with us – we love meeting people and spending time with them, but communication requires mental capacity, and we find ourselves failing to respond to texts, and forgetting birthdays or other important events (not to mention appointments and deadlines).

Use the space below to think about three of the people you love the most and reflect on what you believe they love about you, and what they find frustrating.

_____ loves me because:

....

....

_____ gets cross with me because:

....

....

_____ loves me because:

....

....

_____ gets cross with me because:

....

....

_____ loves me because:

....

....

_____ gets cross with me because:

....

....

The importance of visual reminders

I've experienced similar struggles with family, friends and loved ones – when I can't see them, I almost forget they exist. By keeping visual reminders in our lives, we can not only avoid arguments with those closest to us, but we can also complete more tasks and achieve more success.

Here's a list of possible solutions:

- Whiteboard (with coloured pens for different people or tasks)
- Sticky notes in the place you visit most recently (bathroom, fridge, bed)
- Calendar reminders in your phone
- Alarms on your phone for cut-off times and deadlines.

Below, I want you to get intentional with your strategy for keeping friends and family close – outline what you're going to do and how you're going to do it, and use this journal to check in on your progress in the pages at the end.

Your brain works differently

Like I've already said, the ADHD brain works a little bit differently. We are expected to conform to a 9–5 working pattern, but, for example, my mind is at its best at night. It's when I'm feeling most creative and 'switched on'.

Think about when you feel most creative and alert, when your brain seems to be firing on all cylinders.

Make a note of the time and place/situation, and commit yourself to using that time for planning – use the box below to outline how that looks for you.

Time:

Place/situation:

I will:

Today I am …

....

....

Today, you're going to take some steps towards coming to terms with your diagnosis, and unmasking your authentic self.

Masking and unmasking

People with ADHD are often unsure how to behave in any given situation, especially socially. You'll avoid behaviours that you've seen attract criticism, and instead you'll mirror someone else's behaviours. In this way, you'll be constantly shapeshifting and that's exhausting.

More importantly, if you don't know whether your behaviour is a genuine reflection of your authentic self or an act in order to be likeable, it means you have no idea who you really are.

Take a moment to reflect, and write down below three reasons why you feel the need to conceal your authentic self.

I mask because …

1. ....

....

2. ....

....

3. ....

....

....

Here are some common reasons for masking – you may recognize them:

- You think being vulnerable will be a burden on other people.
- You are terrified of criticism so you put on a likeable persona (this persona can change depending on who you're with).
- You have a deep feeling of being unlikeable so you pretend to be someone else.

Deciding to unmask is a personal decision and one that must be implemented very slowly. It's ultimately a process of self-discovery after years of pretending to be someone else. There is no requirement to unmask in all situations at the same time, and no shame in being inconsistent. Put your own safety first.

Here's a reflective exercise.

Think deeply about the day that's just passed. Ask yourself the following questions and write the answers below each.

1. What happened today that brought me joy?

2. What happened today that made me anxious?

3. What tasks did I enjoy?

4. What tasks frustrated me?

Use this self-awareness to say 'no' more frequently, and the confidence to say 'yes' more often.

Spend time with likeminded people who 'get you', who understand how you think and who you don't feel the need to constantly say 'sorry' to.

Find people who don't tell you to 'calm down' when you're excitedly sharing a story with them.

Find people who skip the small talk and jump straight into the heavy stuff.

Find people who don't ask why you're using a fidget toy.

What will be better when you become your authentic self?

....

....

....

....

....

....

....

....

....

After reading this chapter

ONE THING I WANT TO CHANGE

....

....

....

....

ONE THING I WANT TO DO MORE OF

....

....

....

....

ONE THING I AM GRATEFUL FOR

....

....

....

....

ONE THING TO BE PROUD OF MYSELF FOR

....

....

....

....

2

Finding Your ADHD Strengths

Today I am ...

....

....

Strengths versus struggles

Below is a table with two columns. On the left, list what you believe to be all the negative ADHD traits. On the right, list what you believe to be the positive traits.

Negative	Positive

Which list was longer for you? Many people see ADHD as all struggle, struggle, struggle. It's enough to make anyone feel hopeless. ADHD has its challenges, but there are so many strengths, too. We'll start unpicking these in this chapter. Here are my lists:

Negative	Positive
Struggle to focus	Resilience
Struggle to complete tasks	Creativity
Struggle to pay attention	Problem-solving skills
Struggle with organization	Hyperfocus
Struggle with planning	Calm in a crisis
Struggle with stress	Conversational skills
	Spontaneity
	Entrepreneurial
	Empathic and intuitive
	Sees patterns where others see chaos
	Courageous
	Finds unique solutions to difficult problems
	Can talk about several different topics at once
	High energy
	Willingness to take risks

Note how there are over twice as many positives as negatives! It's so easy to forget about our strengths and to focus on the challenging aspects of ADHD. It's why so many of us struggle with imposter syndrome and self-doubt. We literally forget about our accomplishments. In the next section, we're going to look at some insights and strategies that will help you change how you remember your accomplishments.

Today I am ...

....

....

When an ADHD person accomplishes something, they will quickly move on to the next task (and the next, and the next, and so on), without any pause for reflection and gratitude. While this velocity of accomplishment means we are able to get a lot done in a short amount of time, it can also lead to success amnesia – where we literally forget about our success. So let's look at how we might remember to celebrate our accomplishments (with thanks to the amazing ADHD coach trainer Leanne Maskell, for sharing some of her insights and strategies).

Journaling can be hugely useful. Completing exercises like the one below means that, every time you feel overwhelmed by imposter syndrome, you can use your journal as an evidence book.

Write down three accomplishments from the past week:

1. ....

....

2. ....

....

3. ....

....

Write down your biggest accomplishment from last month:

....

....

At the end of this book, you will find pages devoted to noting your daily and monthly accomplishments – use them!

Celebrating your wins is important, too. Ensure you make time in your calendar to treat yourself – this creates a gap between your accomplishments and builds an association between the achievement and a reward. It also gives you time to reflect on (and be grateful for) your success.

Use the selection in the table below to plan your rewards (substitute your own if you prefer), writing one in each 'Monthly achievement box' at the end of this book.

Make a victory playlist of songs that make you feel happy and confident.	Invent a personal holiday – name a day after yourself and spend the time however you want.
Cook your favourite meal (whether it's pancakes or lasagne).	Go cloud-watching or star-gazing.
Have a 'yes' day (within reason) – say 'yes' to fun, spontaneous things you'd normally put off.	Book a meal in your favourite restaurant.
Buy some new stationery.	Find a new Netflix drama to binge.
Start the hobby you've been meaning to do (with hyperfocus).	Treat yourself to the luxury version of a hot drink from your favourite café.

Write yourself a letter

It is important, during your most vulnerable times, that you remember exactly how strong, capable and awesome you are.

On the next page, you're going to write a letter to the 'you' who has struggled with particular situations, reminding yourself why you're amazing and what your ADHD strengths are that make you so special. This is a task you should return to again and again, particularly during difficult times, and in the morning when you first wake up.

Dear

With all my love,

You have incredible strengths. However, because the world is designed for neurotypical people, it can take longer for you to discover them.

If you display your natural behaviour, you are called 'too much'.

Spend a few minutes listing five negative things you believe about yourself, based on what others have told you:

1. ....

....

....

2. ....

....

....

3. ....

....

....

4. ....

....

5. ....

....

....

The result of all this corrective messaging compounds over time to create a person – you – who has a deep feeling of being different. As a result of this, you have become expert at pretending to be 'normal'. You alter your personality to match who you're with at any given time, and as a result, you have absolutely no idea who you actually are.

In the next pages, we'll help you build self-awareness, so you can better understand your strengths.

Today I am …

....

....

It's possible you have masked for so long that you don't know what's 'you' and what's 'masking'. Once the penny drops and you realize there's a beautiful stranger hiding underneath the mask, you can begin to grow your self-awareness.

Study your knee-jerk reactions

All of us will experience things in our day-to-day that immediately fill us with emotion. It could be intense joy, sadness, anger, excitement, anticipation, nervousness, craving, boredom, desire, relief or many other emotions. It's important to monitor these instant reactions.

Think of a recent occasion when you had an intense emotional reaction. What happened, and how did it make you feel?

....

....

....

....

....

....

If, for example, you wrote down a reaction to someone doing something unethical or rude, that's a strong signal to suggest you find that behaviour disrespectful. Or if you felt happiness immediately after helping someone, that's a strong signal to suggest you're a kind and empathetic person.

Use the journaling pages at the back of this book to make a note of your knee-jerk reactions, and build up a picture of your strengths.

Ask the people you love

Asking a trusted friend or family member for positive feedback is a good way to build self-awareness. Write down below three questions that you would like to ask a person close to you – and commit to asking them.

1. ....
....
....
....

2. ....
....
....
....

3. ....
....
....
....
....

Unmask in private

Finally, if you really want to know what your strengths are, watch yourself when no one else is watching. Become aware of your actions when you're under no pressure to mask. Your ADHD strengths are hiding in plain sight, and when you pay attention, you'll see them.

Today I am …

With great hyperfocus comes a great advantage

One of our biggest strengths is our ability to lose ourselves in focus. We can operate at superhuman levels if we're working on something that excites us. It's important to recognize when you're in a hyperfocus and to know what sorts of activities send you into one. This will build on your self-awareness.

Use the space below to reflect on the most recent occasion when you became hyperfocused – note how it made you feel, and what you achieved.

Make sure you're not burning out

Hyperfocus is brilliant – but it can also interfere with important areas of your life. Hyperfocus makes you, and other people with ADHD, more susceptible to burnout. It's so important to recognize when your body is signalling to you that it needs a break. It's the small signs that perhaps are first to show the effects of burnout – biting your fingernails, or clenching your jaw. They are the early warning signs that you must learn to respect.

What are your 'small signs'? Make a list:

....

....

....

....

....

....

....

....

....

....

....

....

If you are noticing an increase in any of the signs on your list, take your foot off the pedal and take some rest. The hyperfocus will return when you're ready.

Leaning into your ADHD strengths

You probably find that many of your behaviour patterns contradict what society says is 'normal'. Perhaps you don't work best at 'normal' times, or you don't complete your work in advance, or you don't work well in teams. Society tells us we need to analyse every possible outcome before we take action, but perhaps you've tried to do that and it hasn't worked so well for you.

Use the space below to reflect about those areas where 'normal' expectations don't work for you. What would you do differently?

The norm	What works for me

Remember – society begs us to be cautious, but people with ADHD are doers. We create stuff. We start things.

The moment you stop trying to be 'normal' is the moment you embrace your strengths and start to thrive.

After reading this chapter

ONE THING I WANT TO CHANGE

....

....

....

....

....

ONE THING I WANT TO DO MORE OF

....

....

....

....

....

ONE THING I AM GRATEFUL FOR

....

....

....

....

....

ONE THING TO BE PROUD OF MYSELF FOR

....

....

....

....

....

3

Why Does Everybody Hate Me?

Today I am …

....

....

A sensitive child

You've probably experienced **rejection sensitivity dysphoria (RSD)** for as long as you can remember. I can recall feeling it for the first time at four years old when I tried potato printing. The teacher suggested I do it differently for a better effect and I perceived her advice as criticism. I was both heartbroken and furious.

What's your earliest memory of feeling rejected or criticized? How did you react?

....

....

....

....

....

....

....

....

Even the smallest criticisms can be devastating. Someone correcting you; someone who's too busy to see you. It can be almost a physical pain — sometimes even rage. It's an intense emotional reaction which can make you lash out in the moment and say something you regret.

You may well experience RSD on a daily basis, or even more frequently, and later we're going to look at ways you can manage it more successfully.

How does RSD present for you? Reflect in the space below on the way in which it shows up in your adult life, and the emotions you associate with it.

....

....

....

....

....

....

....

....

....

....

....

....

....

....

....

....

....

Scientists are divided over whether RSD is a response from the brain's frontal lobe (the part of the brain which, in our case, may be deficient in the neurotransmitters required to properly regulate emotions) or a response from the brain as it remembers a trauma.

But why can't it be both?

Look at the list below and tick the statements that you've heard used to describe or question your behaviour (either recently or in the past, including as a child):

☐ Why can't you just remember?   ☐ Why are you so disorganized?

☐ Why can't you just be on time?   ☐ Why can't you just focus?

☐ Why are you being weird?   ☐ You're so emotional!

☐ Just plan your time better!   ☐ You procrastinate all the time

☐ You're just being lazy   ☐ You never finish anything

☐ Stop being so clumsy!   ☐ You're so careless

☐ Stop making excuses   ☐ Just try harder!

☐ Why are you so forgetful?   ☐ Stop being odd!

☐ Your room is a mess!   ☐ Stop fidgeting!

☐ You're so impulsive   ☐ Pay attention!

Yes, there is trauma. You have been repeatedly criticized and rejected by your peers. You've been continuously told you're odd, and that makes you feel broken. You're not. You are, instead, haunted by the memory of past criticisms – memories that are embedded in your subconscious, which are triggered whenever you encounter a rejection and which make you instinctively react defensively. We take the first step towards managing RSD when we accept that RSD isn't our fault. Why not? Because being in a constant state of overwhelm isn't a choice.

What does your internal monologue sound like? Write down your most persistent self-critical thoughts here; I've started by sharing two of my own.

1. 'My partner must think I'm so childish.'
2. 'I made such a scene, I'm so embarrassed.'

3. ....

....

....

4. ....

....

....

5. ....

....

....

Now copy out the words beneath, writing them out three times, and make a commitment to bring them to mind when you next hear those thoughts:

IT'S AUTOMATIC, AND IT'S NOT MY FAULT

1. ....

....

2. ....

....

3. ....

....

Today I am …

_____

_____

People pleasing, setting boundaries

The impact of RSD on your behaviours goes further than making you emotionally dysregulated, or reactive, to criticism. When society is unkind, or kids are mean, you will become conditioned to be on alert constantly. As a result, you will be over-vigilant, anticipating further rejection, and continually taking steps to avoid it.

Do you bend over backwards to please everyone?

Are you afraid to say what you think in case it starts an argument?

Do you know how to say 'no'?

Take some time to list below some recent (or less recent) occasions when you've taken steps to avoid conflict or rejection.

....

....

....

....

....

....

....

....

....

Did one of the occasions include your inability to say 'no'? An inability to set boundaries in place will make you feel anxious and overwhelmed.

Times when you said 'yes'	What would happen if you'd said 'no'?

Being a people pleaser will burn you out. It undermines your relationships because it means you are never truly honest with those close to you, and your identity will not feel secure.

First steps to saying 'no'

You don't have to become instantly assertive; you can take small steps to start to create boundaries. Below you'll see two different ways in which you can say 'no' without the confrontation or conflict which makes you uncomfortable.

1. Say, 'Let me think about it.'
2. Send a text message saying, 'Thank you for asking, but unfortunately I don't have time right now.'

Add two of your own suggestions below:

....

....

....

....

....

....

....

....

Refer back to these when you're next tempted to say 'yes'. It might seem like small steps, but this is a huge milestone in your journey towards setting boundaries and establishing self-confidence.

From 'let me think about it' to actual 'no'

On the next page is a space for you to write down a summary of the moments over the next days and weeks when you did actually say 'no'. Making a diary note of that moment will help you remember that point in time and enable you to meditate and reflect on it. Over time your subconscious will recognize that nothing bad happened as a result of you saying 'no', and this will give you the confidence to repeat that behaviour.

I said 'no' when:

Today I am …

....

....

Managing RSD

You can take steps to shield yourself from the damaging effects of RSD, but it's not always possible to avoid a flare-up.

For a short-term strategy, try to snap yourself out of the intensity by forcing your brain to think about something else. Crunching an ice cube, for example, if you're drinking a cold drink at that point in time, or curling your toes really hard.

Write down two RSD flare-up solutions of your own:

1. ....

....

....

....

2. ....

....

....

....

Bring them with you when you next enter a situation which comes with a risk of encountering rejection.

Moving on to the long-term strategies, it's important to look within yourself to examine why you react very intensely when confronted with a rejection. Take a look at the questions on the next page and do your best to answer each one honestly and without shame.

Did someone make you feel worthless a long time ago? How?

....

....

....

....

....

....

Are you working really hard to maintain your self-worth to compensate for that early experience of feeling worthless? How does that manifest?

....

....

....

....

....

....

Do you feel that your self-worth is at stake when someone criticizes you because you have associated your self-worth with how others perceive you? How does that make you feel?

....

....

....

....

....

....

Over time, the answers to these questions can be discovered through therapy. Therapy can help us build a sense of belief and decondition us from our need for external validation to feel worthy.

Take yourself out of the situation

Rather than reacting impulsively to RSD in the moment, train yourself to make 'Give me a minute, please' your default response. After this, be ready with a prepared reason to remove yourself from the situation.

You can also use the pause to remind yourself of your strengths – give yourself positive affirmations, and if you can't remember them, write them down below and refer back to them whenever you need them.

My positive affirmations

I am

I am

I am

I am

I am

I am

I am

I am

I am

I am

If you're unable to put a pause between the stimulus and the reaction (because we're all human and our impulses will get the better of us sometimes), you can mitigate the consequences by using sentences that start with the word 'I', instead of the word 'You'.

Instead of 'You're wrong!' – try 'I don't agree with what you said.'

Instead of 'You're being so unreasonable!' – try 'I feel unfairly treated.'

Activate your five senses

I find that activating all five of my senses helps to distract me, too. You can do this in the moment, but practise below with this written exercise.

Five things I can see

Four things I can touch

Three things I can smell

Two things I can hear

One thing I can taste

It's automatic, and it's not my fault

It's useful to reframe every RSD encounter as being a bit of feedback about a very particular part of you and not a criticism or a rejection of the whole of you. Also, it's massively beneficial to recognize that you don't have all the information and that sometimes there is an innocent reason behind somebody doing something that you thought was a rejection.

Each and every one of us will recognize the horrible feeling that RSD brings. It feels as though we're drowning. It's an insufferable feeling of heartache and pain. Clench your fists. Scream at the wall. Cry. It's okay to feel those feelings. Embrace them. But also know that they don't define you. They are not you. They are a flashback to something horrible that happened a long time ago. They are a memory of being criticized for being different, rejected for being weird and ostracized for not being neurotypical.

None of those things are our fault. We are neurodivergent and we have our own unique strengths.

Take a moment to remind yourself of some of your unique strengths.

After reading this chapter

ONE THING I WANT TO CHANGE

ONE THING I WANT TO DO MORE OF

ONE THING I AM GRATEFUL FOR

ONE THING TO BE PROUD OF MYSELF FOR

4

Finding Ways to Communicate

Today I am …

....

....

When I received my ADHD diagnosis, every failed relationship suddenly made sense. None of those arguments were my fault. None of them were her fault. They all happened because neither of us had a basic awareness of neurodiversity.

How we express ourselves

In this chapter, we're going to look at how you communicate, and particularly at how you communicate love.

I wish I'd known earlier that people with ADHD express their love for someone in unique ways. We might send our partner a love song where the lyrics perfectly articulate how we feel because communicating our feelings more directly is hard and the song does it so well. Or we might infodump, at great detail and length. Or we want to body double or parallel play with our partners (see below for more on this). Or our partner might share a story and we share one back straight away, not because ours is better, but because we were listening and want to show that we relate.

We have many different ways of expressing our love, or communicating more generally, and they might be quite different from the 'normal' ways of doing so.

There is space on the next page for you to reflect on how you express your love, not just for a partner, but for anyone in your life – family, friend, child or pet.

I show love by …

Today I am …

....

....

Communicating our love, and ourselves

Whether you have ADHD or you're living with, are friends with or are related to someone with ADHD, it's important to have awareness of the unique ways ADHD can show up in your relationships. The ADHD brain often has executive function struggles which mean date nights might be difficult to plan, birthdays might be forgotten, and that thing they wanted for Christmas might not actually get bought.

Normal expectations of love	How does this feel for you?
Long, heartfelt conversations	
Romantic meals together	
Carefully planned surprises	
Giving thoughtful gifts	
Making future plans together	

If the more 'normal' ways of communicating and of showing love appeal to you, that's great. But many people with ADHD find these things make them quite anxious.

We're going to help you explore different ways of communicating that might work better for your relationships.

Infodumping

Infodumping is when we share a lot of information about our special interest. It might sound like you're talking at breakneck speed, but it's your preferred conversation style. Small talk probably makes you anxious or overwhelmed, but Infodumping lets you speak continuously until you've said everything you want to say. But Infodumping does need you to be in a *safe space*, feeling able to communicate without fear of judgement, so take a moment to think about what a safe space might look like for you.

My safe space is …

....

....

....

....

....

....

Remember, too, that an Infodump can happen at any time. For many, communicating during mealtimes or when arriving home from work is 'normal', but as an ADHD person you might find yourself burned out or frazzled at those times, and preferring to sit in silence.

When do you find yourself feeling most burned out?

I feel burned out or shut down when:

Times	Places

If you find yourself needing time to transition from one activity to another, or from work to home, remember what you've written down above and don't force yourself to communicate at what are considered 'normal' times.

Sometimes, you'll have an urge to infodump but the other person's energy isn't in sync. When this happens, it's useful to have a safe word that the non-willing partner can use to communicate their position without triggering an RSD flare-up in the other.

Safe word or phrase:

If this happens, you can still infodump in your journal – use the space below when you need it.

Today I am …

....

....

Body doubling

Related to communication, you may find you can build closeness and partnerships through body doubling. Body doubling is the act of performing a task with somebody else. The other person could either be helping you or simply keeping you company. This creates a strange but extremely effective type of accountability that helps us start and finish tasks. The other person could be with you 'in person' or virtually via a webcam.

Body doubling could be used with family and friends for things such as:

- emptying the washing machine
- checking your finances
- cleaning
- cooking.

And with your partner for:

- brushing your teeth
- taking a shower
- making the bed.

We act differently when we know we're being watched. We feel a subconscious desire to please the other person and this gives us the motivation to do a task that we would otherwise find extremely challenging. Body doubling offers us support with executive function, and the net result is not only tasks completed, but a new closeness and improved communication with the loved one you body double with.

On the next page, spend ten minutes listing the things you would like to do with a body double and reflect on who you'd like to share that time with.

Body doubling when I …

With …

Today I am …

....

....

Unmasked love

ADHDers are impulsive, and our preferred style of communicating how we feel is 'act first, think later'. Our displays of love might be spontaneous and unpredictable. Ideas might come into our minds that cause us to instantly jump up and act on our latest thought, whatever that means.

A show of impulsive happiness means that we feel safe and loved. We've spent a lifetime hiding our true self and pretending to be 'normal'.

What does the definition of true ADHD love look like to you?

Being loved with my ADHD means I can …

....

....

....

....

....

....

....

....

....

....

....

Being loved with your ADHD (not despite it) means understanding one another's brains.

What would you like your loved ones, or your partner, to know about your ADHD brain?

....

....

....

....

....

....

....

....

....

....

....

....

....

....

....

....

....

....

Would you consider showing them this?

ADHD-friendly communication styles

Set aside time every day or week to communicate with your family or partner in a meaningful way. For an ADHD person, 'meaningful' means absorbing what is being said, and responding in a way that doesn't feel forced or contrived.

Communicate in a way that works for you. Here are some examples:

- Having a meaningful conversations when your body is preoccupied with a task.
- Communicating when you're driving, jogging or cleaning.

I communicate best when I am:

Creating solutions; doing acts of service

Ways of showing your love, and feeling loved, can be much more creative than the traditional ones we mentioned at the beginning of this chapter.

For example, when you go out to a restaurant, your partner might recognize that you're feeling anxious and order for you. Or you might be overwhelmed by the menu, so your partner can remind you of meals you have enjoyed in the past.

Buying or creating innovative solutions for your partner's challenges is a beautiful way to demonstrate your love for them. 'I researched your problem, and here are some solutions' translates into 'I love you' for an ADHD person.

Ultimately, an ADHD relationship flourishes when there is understanding, acceptance and a complete removal of shame. That's the key. It all starts with awareness.

On the following page, you will find two spaces. In the first space, write down your thoughts about how your partner, or your family, or your friend, could show their love for you – what does love mean to you? In the second space, write down ways in which you might show your love for them.

Commit to doing these things, and think about how you might make your own needs heard as well.

Things I would like my loved ones to do for me:

Things I would like to do for my loved ones:

After reading this chapter

ONE THING I WANT TO CHANGE

ONE THING I WANT TO DO MORE OF

ONE THING I AM GRATEFUL FOR

ONE THING TO BE PROUD OF MYSELF FOR

5

Making Relationships Work

Today I am ...

....

....

The early stages of a relationship where one or both people have ADHD can be incredibly intense. People are very sure that they've found their soulmate and this person is what they've been looking for. It can be almost too intense to bear.

Think back to some of your earlier relationships. Write down some thoughts on how those relationships felt at the beginning.

....

....

....

....

....

....

....

....

....

....

....

....

....

This early intensity, especially in ADHD relationships, can last quite a while. Whether love develops out of it, or not, is different for everyone. However, nobody can live in this state for ever. Something will eventually break it.

Reflect below on some of the causes of your earlier relationships ending. Make a note of how you felt your ADHD may or may not have contributed.

Today I am …

....

....

Communicating, with love

As we have already explored, much of the success of a relationship where one or both partners has ADHD relies on communication. The most important step couples can take is to recognize where the communication is going wrong. You need a basic awareness of each other's triggers; otherwise you're setting yourself up for a turbulent time.

Five things that trigger me (in relationships):

....

....

....

....

....

....

....

....

....

....

....

....

....

....

As someone with ADHD, once you are triggered, your executive function begins to malfunction and, for you, the conversation stops immediately. From that point, you've got two people having very separate conversations. Your partner continues with the conversation, while you are now ruminating and raging over the trigger, stuck in 'fight or flight' mode.

It's really useful to have a way of communicating when the trigger has occurred. This can be a simple hand signal, a verbal sign, or a code word you can use when you're with other people.

My trigger sign is:

Once you're feeling calmer, have a conversation with your partner about the event. Over time, your conversations will build up a store of knowledge about what your triggers are and how to avoid them going forward.

There will be times, however, when you say something you regret, or which hurts your partner, when you couldn't control your reaction in the heat of the moment. Apologizing is always the first thing you should do in this situation, but you will find that, in the long term, your partner will be more empathetic towards you if you, likewise, understand their neurotype – it's a two-way process.

My partner is …

… happiest when they

....
....
....

… most frustrated when they

....
....
....

… made sad by

....
....
....

… anxious about

....
....
....

My partner doesn't like doing

....
....
....

My partner likes doing

....
....
....

Weekly check-ins can also help keep you both connected. Here are some prompts you can complete here and revisit elsewhere:

What happened this week that made you happy?	
What did I do this week to make you feel close to me?	
Have you learned anything new this week you'd like to share?	
What do you need from me right now (that I'm not giving you)?	
What is your favourite thing about our relationship?	
Is there anything new you'd like us to try together?	
Have you been feeling anxious this week?	
How's your mental health today?	

Today I am …

....

....

Coping with challenges

The ADHD relationships with the highest success rates are the ones where both partners want to work and learn. But what are the signs that things aren't going well, and what can you do to make it better? Let's look at ways in which you can address the things that might be causing problems in your ADHD relationship without you knowing.

Rejection sensitive dysphoria

If RSD is an issue in your relationship, one thing you can both do is to adopt an approach that's supportive of mini-achievements. Create space to celebrate your partner's achievements each week and have them do the same for you. Use the space below to start, and find a place for this in your journal, weekly.

_____

Three great things I did this week:

1. ....

....

2. ....

....

3. ....

....

_____

Affection and touch

It's a nice idea to create little moments of physical touch to make your partner feel safe. For example, a hand on the lap when watching a film or an intentional hug when you arrive home from work.

For me, a loving touch means

....

....

....

....

....

....

Micro check-ins

Even if your questions get a generic response, such as 'I'm okay today, thank you', they remind your partner that you care.

Five ways I will check in with my partner:

1. ....

....

2. ....

....

3. ....

....

4. ....

....

5. ....

....

Allow for hyperfocus

People with ADHD find it hard to instantly transition from one task to another, and breaking hyperfocus can cause arguments when one partner can't make the switch.

Use the space below to note some easy ways of helping you transition from one task to another that you can share with your partner.

When you need me to switch focus, please:

....

....

....

....

....

Allow for decompression

Your partner may not be aware that, by the time you come home from work, you're exhausted – and you need time to decompress. Make a note below of how you do this, so they understand, and include a code word or phrase so they know this is the case.

When I arrive home, I relax and decompress by:

....

....

....

....

....

Code word/phrase

....

....

....

As ever, communication is key

When one or both partners have ADHD, it's easy for impulsive reactions to escalate into instant arguments. It's important to communicate in those moments, so that each of you knows what is happening and that one or both of you is not emotionally regulated.

Finally, it's vital to acknowledge that arguments happen from time to time, and they may be started by you. This is normal and no cause for shame. Follow them with an honest conversation, and you can use the experience as an opportunity to understand each other's behaviour and to grow as a couple.

Where do you see your relationship in 12 months/3 years/5 years?
12 months

....

....

....

....

3 years

....

....

....

....

5 years

....

....

....

....

Today I am …

....

....

Self-worth is key

A feeling of low self-worth is likely to be ingrained in your subconscious, causing a part of you to self-sabotage meaningful relationships because you think you don't deserve to have them.

To shut down your subconscious desire to self-sabotage, it's vital that you're aware of it, and that you take steps to take away its power. This can be done by focusing on the evidence you have that contradicts it – and you have a lot of evidence.

Remember that journaling, meditation and breathwork can help override your subconscious feeling of 'I'm not good enough'. We've already discussed an achievement list, but you can't make too many.

Things I've achieved this week:

1. ....

....

2. ....

....

3. ....

....

4. ....

....

5. ....

....

Looking for novelty

Lots of people with ADHD crave novelty, and it may mean you find yourself struggling after the honeymoon period and looking for a new relationship. Rather than accepting this as inevitable, think about how you might maintain some sparks of that initial feeling of joy, so you don't start to feel compelled to leave the relationship.

Three new things to enjoy together:

1. ....

....

....

2. ....

....

....

3. ....

....

....

It is true that you will lose some of that dopamine after spending lots of time with the other person. Instead of looking for it elsewhere, use the connections you are making with the help of this journal to replace it with oxytocin instead – the chemical released when we form a close bond with someone we love; our body's reward to us for becoming vulnerable and connecting deeply with another.

Things I want my partner to know about me and my ADHD

Use the prompts below to explore three specific ADHD traits, and how they might impact on your relationship, so you can talk openly about challenges going forward.

What I might do	How it manifests, how you might help
1. Catastrophize over our relationship	
2. Do unusual things at unusual times	
3. Say things on impulse and out of the blue	

Whatever happens, good or bad, always take the time together to retrospectively analyse the event, communicate your findings with each other, and use them to grow your mutual understanding of how the other's brain works.

You are each other's centrepiece. You are each other's travelling companion.

And what a journey it's going to be.

After reading this chapter

ONE THING I WANT TO CHANGE

ONE THING I WANT TO DO MORE OF

ONE THING I AM GRATEFUL FOR

ONE THING TO BE PROUD OF MYSELF FOR

6

Being, or Becoming, a Parent

Today I am ...

....

....

This part of your journal will help you focus on what might be needed to be a parent. You may be considering becoming a parent (one day, or sooner), you may be a parent already, or it may be that pets are your children currently. Some sections will be more applicable to you than others, but it is worthwhile to look at each one and consider your relationship with your possible future child, your existing child, or any creature you share your life with and care for.

How did, or do, you picture yourself as a parent (before becoming one)?

....

....

....

....

....

....

....

....

....

....

Reflecting on how you thought you would be (or how you think you will be) as a parent probably makes you feel a level of frustration or sadness at the perceived additional challenges of parenting with ADHD. You're probably already aware of how much you sometimes struggle to manage your own schedule, diet and wellbeing – let alone being, as a parent or carer, responsible for someone else's. You are likely to be facing additional pressures that come from your own ADHD neurotype, let alone those of your child or future child (who may or may not have that archetype).

How do you think your ADHD does, or will, affect the way you parent your child (or care for your pet, if relevant)?

My ADHD affects my parenting because:

....

....

....

....

....

....

....

....

....

....

....

....

....

....

....

Let's take some time to think about how behaviours associated with ADHD may be holding you back from being the parent you want to be (reminder: trying new things is great, but you are already good enough).

Perfectionism

If you have internalized the messages about not being 'good enough', then being a perfectionist might sound like an attractive quality, but in reality it can lead to obsessive behaviour that impacts your mental health and contributes to your sense of shame or failure.

The main way to make marginal improvements to your perfectionism is to be intentionally imperfect – and record the results.

Try this exercise next time you're trying to be 'perfect'.

I wanted to ... [deliver the work early/check it again]

....

....

....

Instead, I ...

....

....

....

The result was ...

....

....

....

The difference between the imperfect outcome and the perfect outcome will be minuscule. However, the difference in your mental health, energy levels and general wellbeing will be vast.

Overwhelm

It is very easy, as a parent (or a future parent), to become overwhelmed by the thought – and, of course, the reality – of caring for a baby.

The exercises below are designed to help you address ADHD overwhelm if you are already a parent (with a reminder to seek professional help if it is all getting too much to cope with), or to think about what your strategies might be were you to become one.

1. Self-care: How could you manage your ADHD scaffolding (exercise, meditation) in a way that works round your child's routine?

....

....

....

....

....

2. Be proud of yourself. List five positive affirmations:

....

....

....

....

....

3. Seek help when you need it. Write down one person and two things that might offer support when you're overwhelmed:

....

....

....

....

....

Today I am …

....

....

Bonding

Whether they have ADHD or not, there is no doubt that children feel most secure when they are bonded to their parent and experience strong, enduring connections. It's so important to let your child know you have their back, no matter what.

I will deepen my connection with my child by:

....

....

....

....

....

....

....

....

....

....

....

....

....

Remember, a visual representation of your love (a sticky note, a teddy, a special stone they can keep with them) can really deepen your connection, especially if you or child struggle with articulating your emotions.

Routine and space

Creating a routine that allows you very short bursts of restorative space and time, and to rebalance, will be critical. Using the prompts given below, structure something that could work for you, or that you could implement now if appropriate.

Movement	
Early-morning routine	
Evening routine (e.g. a bath, reading)	
Mental and physical relaxation (e.g. stretching, meditation)	

It's the intention that really matters, and that is to create a moment, no matter how small, where you can focus on nothing but the moment and relax. These little moments are really important because they provide a pause between the demands of parenthood and therefore help minimize the feelings of overwhelm.

Today I am …

....

....

The worst thing you can do to an ADHD kid is to try to turn them into a neurotypical kid or bring them closer to a neurotypical one.

Let's explore ways of working with your ADHD child if you are already a parent.

1. Physical activity – what does this look like for your child?

....

....

....

2. Hobbies that engross them – what does this look like for your child?

....

....

....

3. Praising them for effort not reward – when can you praise your child?

....

....

....

4. Body doubling – when can you body double with your child?

....

....

....

5. Connecting with other parents of ADHD kids – who do you know?

....

....

....

How to interact with an ADHD child's brain

There are two ways of interacting with your child that avoids them feeling criticized and puts them in control.

Asking questions. What are the situations when a question would work better than a demand?

....

....

....

....

....

....

....

....

Making choices. What are the situations when a choice would work better than a decision made for them?

....

....

....

....

....

....

....

....

....

....

....

Don't sweat the small stuff

When we stop thinking the traditional way is the right way, we can begin to make simple accommodations within our households that will make for a happier environment.

Small stuff	Big stuff
e.g. elbows on the table, sitting up straight	e.g. my child being fed and happy

After reading this chapter

ONE THING I WANT TO CHANGE

ONE THING I WANT TO DO MORE OF

ONE THING I AM GRATEFUL FOR

ONE THING TO BE PROUD OF MYSELF FOR

7

ADHD at Work
The Entrepreneur Brain

Today I am ...

....

....

What ADHD strengths do you bring to the workplace?

I am ...

....

....

....

....

....

....

....

....

....

....

....

....

What aspects of the workplace do you find difficult?

I don't like/can't cope with …

....

....

....

....

....

....

....

....

....

....

....

....

....

....

....

....

....

You don't need a diagnosis to be entitled to workplace accommodations. You simply need to show that your anxiety is substantially affecting your ability to do your job.

You may want to return to the entry you created above and make a further record of things that are proving difficult, so you have evidence in addition to a doctor's note.

Understanding your ADHD brain

The more you are able to grow your understanding of your ADHD brain, the more you will be able to harness its powers and find yourself comfortable asking for important but easy-to-implement changes.

Which of the following accommodations would you find helpful?

☐ Working from home

☐ Earlier or later start times

☐ Noise-cancelling headphones

☐ Fidget toys/sensory support

☐ ADHD coaching

☐ Written notes after meetings

☐ Regular breaks

☐ A quiet space

☐ Body doubling

☐ Step-by-step instructions

☐ Visual reminders

☐ A building map

☐ Anything else

Using your emergent awareness of your strengths and struggles in the workplace, and the list above, you can begin to build a picture of a workplace that works for you, and to discuss it with your manager and human resources team.

Use the space below to reflect on the last meeting you attended.

What I found useful …

What I found unhelpful …

What I found difficult …

How I'd prefer to do it …

First, ask whether a meeting is really necessary. If it is, ask for the agenda in advance and ask whether the organizers will brief everyone to submit ideas/solutions/discussions 24 hours in advance – so that every voice is heard, including yours.

Today I am …

....

....

Entrepreneurs

Research shows that people with ADHD are far more likely to start a business; we are natural entrepreneurs. Our internal desire to create stuff, combined with an attitude to risk that many others might try to subdue makes us the perfect candidates to start companies. We're great at spotting trends, we're calm in a crisis, and our out-of-the-box thinking enables us to see opportunities that others miss. And our most successful projects are those which connect with our core motivations.

What are your core motivations?

....

....

....

....

....

....

....

....

....

....

....

....

....

....

If you weren't sure what to put as your core motivations on the previous page, you can speed up the process by journaling further or through meditation. If you are looking to start a business, though, try the Idea Shelf first.

Put your new ideas on the Idea Shelves below:

If after two weeks you're still excited about any idea you put on a shelf, you can take it 'down' and begin working on it. By delaying slightly, you'll find out if the idea truly connects with your core motivations and you'll save yourself huge amounts of time and money.

Finding your 'WHY' is absolutely essential for making a success of any new business opportunity.

Getting started

If you are struggling with procrastination and putting off getting started, reflect on your 'why'. Hyperfocus on it. Read your journal entries to see it written down. Zoom in on it, and often this will get you over the procrastination hump and keep you motivated.

You will also need to be open to the skills and strengths that you have – and those that you will need to delegate.

Skills I have

....

....

....

....

....

Skills I don't have (yet)

....

....

....

....

....

Looking at the skills you don't yet have, reflect on those you can treat as mini-projects or quests. However, don't get distracted or sidetracked by them if they don't align with your business goals, and don't forget to delegate when you need to.

Disrupt the routine

If boredom is threatening to derail your plans – or if you're fearing burnout – it's important to remember to keep all areas of your life fresh and interesting by introducing new things. They don't need to be big changes, but anything that can switch up your routine or bring new interest will help keep you on track.

Five things I will do to switch up my routine:

1. ....

....

....

2. ....

....

....

3. ....

....

....

4. ....

....

....

5. ....

....

....

The key is to pattern interrupt your central nervous system, which will ensure you stay engaged with your new business idea.

Today I am …

....

....

If the idea of KPIs (key performance indicators) makes you want to scream, you might want to think about different ways of incentivizing yourself – particularly gamifying.

Outline three key milestones and your reward for each:

Milestone 1
Reward:

....

....

Milestone 2
Reward:

....

....

Milestone 3
Reward:

....

....

The rewards don't have to be huge, just enough to drive that feeling of success and achievement.

A point-scoring system can also help overcome any struggles with task initiation and procrastination.

Add your own tasks and points to the list below:

Reading emails	2 points
Answering emails	5 points
Calling a client	10 points
Writing an invoice	25 points
	___ points
	___ points
	___ points
	___ points
	___ points

Grade the activity according to how you feel – you can double or even triple your points if you are feeling overwhelmed or anxious.

You also need to incentivize yourself to take breaks, and to take the relevant steps to manage anxiety or burnout, so give yourself points for the relevant breathing, meditation or relaxation exercises.

My reward for:

....

100 points

....

250 points

....

500 points

Accountability

Accountability should be a driving force behind your business endeavours. Creating goals and check-ins that are open for all to see will help you stay motivated, focused and on track. Accountability creates short-term consequences when you don't complete something (having a 'buddy' is a good way of creating these consequences).

Use the space below to outline three different ways in which you will create accountability for yourself:

I will create accountability by:

1. ....

....

....

2. ....

....

....

3. ....

....

....

Personal development

It's very easy for us ADHDers to go full steam ahead towards our business goals, but we need to find time to maintain our Personal Development Plan (PDP). This should look like a pyramid with three levels. The bottom level, the widest one, is called 'Self-awareness'. The middle level is called 'Action' and the top level is called 'Goals'. The bottom and top levels, our self-awareness and goals, always need to be aligned, while the action is what we need to do in order to achieve our goals.

Your PDP

GOALS

....

....

....

ACTION

....

....

....

SELF-AWARENESS

....

....

....

Working on your self-awareness will keep you aware of your core values. If you don't work on your self-awareness, your core values might change and they won't be aligned to your goals anymore – and that's when times get hard.

Today I am …

....

....

You might find that you're not yet embedded with your self-awareness, and you may need to do more work on this.

Reflect on a recent professional social encounter. Did you feel undermined or empowered? Anxious or confident? Deflated or motivated?
Write down your thoughts here and take care to reflect on them from time to time.

....

....

....

....

....

....

....

....

....

....

If you are struggling, make some adjustments to your middle pyramid layer (actions) to keep everything aligned.

After reading this chapter

ONE THING I WANT TO CHANGE

....

....

....

....

ONE THING I WANT TO DO MORE OF

....

....

....

....

ONE THING I AM GRATEFUL FOR

....

....

....

....

ONE THING TO BE PROUD OF MYSELF FOR

....

....

....

....

8

Coping with the ADHD Tax

Today I am …

....
....

Use the space below to calculate what you've paid this month in ADHD tax:

....
....
....
....
....
....
....
....
....
....
....
....
....
....

Let's face it. People with ADHD are great for the economy. But there is an underlying reason in our brains for this behaviour and there are real strategies to manage it.

The next time you want to buy something on impulse, use the space below to write down why you want it, what it will do to make your life better, and what's so special about it.

My next purchase will:

....

....

....

....

....

....

....

....

....

....

....

....

....

....

Infodumping your excitement can give you lots of dopamine and distract you from buying the thing you're craving. You might even find you have received all the dopamine you need, and you no longer feel compelled to actually buy the thing.

You may also find it useful to list the times when you want to spend money — and the times when you don't.

I spend money when ...	I don't spend money when ...

It is very likely that situations when you don't spend money provide you with lots of dopamine, meaning you don't feel the urge to hunt for it elsewhere. You don't impulse spend because you need the thing, you impulse spend because you want to feel something.

You can also seek stimulation from, for example:

- playing computer games
- calling a friend
- using a fidget toy.

Ten things I can do to keep my brain happy:

1. ....

2. ....

3. ....

4. ....

5. ....

6. ....

7. ....

8. ....

9. ....

10. ....

Using your list, and the suggestions given here for when you're tempted to buy something on impulse, you will be able to keep your brain happy, engaged and stimulated enough to avoid the need to seek dopamine through impulsive purchases.

You can also try holding your breath when you're faced with something you're desperate to buy. Hold it for as long as you can, and focus on the first 30 seconds of euphoria and then the growing feeling of discomfort. This will displace the urge to purchase and distract you until the moment has passed.

Today I am …

....

....

Do it now – stop procrastinating

Procrastination is what doubles the parking fines or increases the interest on your credit card bill.

Use this space to reflect on the last time you procrastinated, and the outcome:

....

....

....

....

....

....

....

....

....

....

....

....

....

....

In future, connecting with memories in this way will help you pay your tickets and bills immediately, avoiding the shame.

Paying the tax upfront

Sometimes it's better to pay more for something for the sake of convenience than it is to pay less for something that you will not use.

For example:

Whole cauliflower	£0.50	Pre-chopped vegetables	£2.50
Whole broccoli	£0.50		
	= £1.00		= £2.50

The ADHD tax on buying the whole vegetables is £1.50 because they were all wasted, but the ADHD tax on the pre-cut vegetables is only £1.00 because that's the cost of convenience.

Five more ways you can pay the tax upfront:

1. ....

2. ....

3. ....

4. ....

5. ....

Bear in mind that the monetary cost isn't the only thing to consider – you also need to consider the cost of your energy. If the equation is **Financial cost + Energy cost = Total cost of purchase**, then sometimes purchasing pre-cut vegetables is actually cheaper because it has a lower total cost.

Try this simple six-month budget template. Customize it in your journal pages if necessary to fit your own spending patterns.

	JAN	FEB
INCOME		
Salary/wages		
Miscellaneous		
TOTAL		
EXPENSES		
Home/utilities		
Food		
Entertainment		
Transportation		
Holidays		
Personal		
TOTAL		

	MARCH	APRIL
INCOME		
Salary/wages		
Miscellaneous		
TOTAL		
Expenses		
Home/utilities		
Food		
Entertainment		
Transportation		
Holidays		
Personal		
TOTAL		

	MAY	JUNE
INCOME		
Salary/wages		
Miscellaneous		
TOTAL		
Expenses		
Home/utilities		
Food		
Entertainment		
Transportation		
Holidays		
Personal		
TOTAL		

After reading this chapter

ONE THING I WANT TO CHANGE

ONE THING I WANT TO DO MORE OF

ONE THING I AM GRATEFUL FOR

ONE THING TO BE PROUD OF MYSELF FOR

9

Tough Times
Addictions and Burnout

Today I am …

....

....

Having ADHD brings great strengths, but it also brings a susceptibility to burnout and addictive behaviours; the following pages are designed to help you begin to manage those, or even to avoid them.

Burnout

Hyperfocus is one of the reasons people with ADHD are more susceptible to burnout. Before you get there, your body will start sending signals that you need to take your foot off the pedal.

In the space below, make a list of the physical signs and symptoms you think might indicate you are approaching burnout:

....

....

....

....

....

....

....

....

....

There are many things that will help you manage burnout (and lots of excellent resources for this): make sure you get plenty of sleep, spend quality time with people away from work, get outside, be active, eat well and practise mindfulness. Most important, however, is paying attention to the small things – crying for no reason, for example, or biting your nails, or clenching your jaw.

Thinking about the 'small signs' of burnout, what might yours be?

....

....

....

....

....

....

....

Using a journal to record your mood fluctuations, your triggers and your patterns of behaviour will help you manage burnout or approach burnout more effectively.

Saying 'no' will also help; you can use the 24-hour rule to do this more effectively, if you like, by letting people know you will get back to them in 24 hours (with a 'no', probably).

My 'saying no' script:

....

....

....

....

....

Today I am …

Addictions

Use the space below to reflect on which of your behaviours you would consider addictive, and what your history of addiction looks like:

People with ADHD have a deficit of dopamine in their prefrontal cortex, which makes it difficult for them to regulate their emotions or to act out executive functions. Essentially, this means you are predisposed to becoming addicted to substances that give you dopamine, such as alcohol, or one of many other drugs. This same deficit makes us more susceptible to pleasure-seeking activities. In simple terms, it makes us extremely impulsive.

How to know if you are powerless over alcohol:

Ask yourself when you reach for a wine bottle, are you drinking because you …

… want to drink it?

....

....

… can't stop drinking it?

....

....

Is your drinking affecting …

… your work?

....

....

… your relationships?

....

....

… your friendships?

....

....

If your drinking is having a detrimental effect on any of the above, it may be an indicator that alcohol is doing you more harm than good.

Remind yourself of your 'why'

Create a diary listing all the memories you have of feeling hungover.

When I drank	
How I felt	
How it affected others	
When I drank	
How I felt	
How it affected others	
When I drank	
How I felt	
How it affected others	
When I drank	
How I felt	
How it affected others	
When I drank	
How I felt	
How it affected others	

The opposite of addiction is connection. Find a community that supports you – build a supportive network of people you trust, and don't try to 'do it' alone.

If you try to 'do it' alone, the demons will creep back. At some point life will get too much and it will be too easy to default to the old habits. So:

1. Admit it.

2. Connect with people.

3. Keep reminding yourself 'why' you stopped.

4. Pick up the phone before you pick up a drink.

Three rules I will make for myself when people say, 'Just have one!'

1. ....

....

....

....

2. ....

....

....

....

3. ....

....

....

....

Think about:

- resolving not to drink before you even leave the house
- planning something you can't do with a hangover
- choosing a trusted friend to support you in your decision not to drink
- deciding your non-alcoholic drink order before you leave the house and having an exit plan.

Alcohol will mute your ADHD positives and amplify the struggles. So, let's remember how exactly this will look:

When I am sober, I am:

When I have been drinking, I am:

It's possible that you've skipped through this section and are thinking that this isn't you, and you don't have a problem with alcohol or any other substance. But ADHD creates stubbornness and a resistance to authority that serves you well in many situations but also makes it hard for you to recognize your own liabilities.

Use the chart below to try and keep a really honest assessment of your intake over two weeks, and return to the start of this chapter if necessary.

Day	Units	Situation
Monday		
Tuesday		
Wednesday		
Thursday		
Friday		
Saturday		
Sunday		
Monday		
Tuesday		
Wednesday		
Thursday		
Friday		
Saturday		
Sunday		

Alcohol probably isn't for you. It's not a good mix with your brain type. Some people can drink and it's okay. Some people can't. There's no shame in being one of the people who can't. You have ADHD and that means you can do things lots of other people can't do. Focus on those things. Focus on being brilliant. Focus on being you. You are enough.

Ten things about my ADHD that are better than alcohol:

1. ....

....

2. ....

....

3. ....

....

4. ....

....

5. ....

....

6. ....

....

7. ....

....

8. ....

....

9. ....

....

10. ....

....

After reading this chapter

ONE THING I WANT TO CHANGE

ONE THING I WANT TO DO MORE OF

ONE THING I AM GRATEFUL FOR

ONE THING TO BE PROUD OF MYSELF FOR

10

Learning to Love Yourself

Today I am …

....

....

You've made it so far through this guided journal – well done! This last part will build on everything you've worked through so far and help you become your own best advocate. Hopefully the work that you've done so well will help you challenge the many negative things you've heard about yourself over the years since your childhood.

What they said	What you know now
You're just lazy!	
I wish you'd apply yourself.	
Just go to bed earlier!	
Why are you so forgetful?	
You're so dramatic!	
You just need to try harder.	

Remember, none of the negative comments are true. You are not lazy or bad – these things are not a choice, and if understood properly, they could be some of your greatest strengths.

Misconceptions

Having ADHD doesn't mean you're hyperactive; in fact, women and girls with ADHD present very differently from men and boys. If you're a woman, you have probably become good at hiding your ADHD, or you may have been misdiagnosed with anxiety, depression or PMS. And even if you're male, ADHD doesn't mean you're necessarily physically hyperactive – it is entirely possible for the hyperactivity to be completely in your head.

What do you think are the biggest misconceptions about ADHD?

....

....

....

....

....

How do these misconceptions make you feel?

....

....

....

....

....

If you've started to unmask as a result of the work you've done here, that's a fantastic start. You've begun a fascinating journey of self-discovery, and all the exciting things are ahead of you. Now everything in your past makes sense. You were always enough.

Today I am …

....

....

Knowing what you do now about ADHD, what would you like to say to your younger self, who's struggling with a sense of feeling different, or of being constantly criticized? Write a short letter to them below.

Dear

....

....

....

....

....

....

....

....

....

....

....

....

....

With love,

....

As your self-awareness grows, you'll find yourself increasingly embracing your ADHD. Along with this, you may even find you realize the importance of finding humour in the more challenging aspects of ADHD.

Can you think of three occasions when your ADHD has created comedy?

1. ....
....
....
....
....

2. ....
....
....
....
....

3. ....
....
....
....
....
....

It's important for you to realize that there is no shame in any of the behaviours or situations you've described above – look at them through the ADHD lens instead, and remember: it's not your fault (and you're not harming anyone!).

With ADHD, it's likely that you find many things easy that others find challenging, and vice versa. Let's take a moment to reflect on your unique strengths (and what doesn't come so easily to you).

What others find hard	What I find easy

What others find easy	What I find hard

Embrace your differences

Like so many of us, your ADHD shows up in mysterious ways – and it's time to fully embrace your differences.

ADHD perhaps makes you struggle with the 'boring stuff' – but let's look at the strengths it brings.

My ADHD makes me:

....

....

....

....

....

....

....

....

....

....

....

....

Today I am …

....

....

It is likely that your ADHD shows up in many amazing (and often contradictory) ways.

Three challenges my ADHD has created this week:

1. ....

....

....

....

....

2. ....

....

....

....

....

3. ....

....

....

....

....

Three opportunities my ADHD has created this week

1. ....

....

....

....

....

2. ....

....

....

....

....

3. ....

....

....

....

....

ADHD has its challenges. The ADHD tax is real. But it's also enabling you to do amazing things.

Hopefully your feelings about your ADHD are changing and evolving as you work through this book and continue with your journal.

How I felt about my ADHD before I started this work:

....

....

....

....

....

....

....

How I feel about my ADHD now:

....

....

....

....

....

....

....

Your mind isn't suited to 'conventional' working practices, and when you fully understand this you will thrive, both professionally and personally.

Remember, the moment you stop trying to be 'normal' is the moment you start to shine.

Today I am ...

....

....

A final takeaway: top ADHD hacks

DOUBLE CHECK: everything, all the time

A WALL OF POCKETS: a pocket hanger for everything near the front door

PLAN YOUR DAY THE NIGHT BEFORE: especially if your night brain is better than your morning brain

KEEP SHOPPING BAGS IN THE CAR: or you'll just keep buying them

BUY PRE-CHOPPED EVERYTHING: it's not more expensive if you actually use them

KEEP A TOOTHBRUSH NEXT TO YOUR BED: brushing with a dry brush is better than nothing, if you keep forgetting

ORGANIZE THE FLOORDROBE: three baskets, labelled 'dirty', 'clean', 'not dirty or clean'

DON'T MAKE CLEANING HARDER: store cleaning products in the room you'll use them in

DON'T EMPTY YOUR DISHWASHER: take the clean plates out when you need them

UPSTAIRS/DOWNSTAIRS: have all the important things (vacuum cleaner, scissors, sticky tape and so on) on both floors (if you have two)

HOOKS INSTEAD OF HANGERS: so much easier

FINISH IT, THROW IT, BIN IT: put empty shower gel bottles on the bathroom floor when you're done, then you'll remember to throw them away

FIGHT THE URGE TO SIT DOWN IMMEDIATELY: maintain your momentum, if you can

IF I DON'T WRITE IT DOWN, IT DOESN'T EXIST: write *everything* down

THE TASK BRACELET SYSTEM: assign a task to a single bracelet (buy or make a pack) and wear each one when you did to get that job done

DON'T RELY ON YOUR BRAIN TO MONITOR TIME: use a timer for everything

IGNORE THE 'COMMON SENSE' STUFF: only do it if it works for you

RUN/WALK/MOVE: exercise is the best thing for the ADHD mind

PROTEIN FOR LUNCH, CARBS FOR DINNER: to keep your brain sharper during the day

THROW STUFF AWAY: try not to hoard, however tempting

TAKE BREAKS FROM SOCIAL MEDIA: try to at least limit your usage – you wouldn't let 100 people into your bedroom, so don't let them into your mind.

Add your own hacks here:

After reading this chapter

ONE THING I WANT TO CHANGE

....

....

....

....

ONE THING I WANT TO DO MORE OF

....

....

....

....

ONE THING I AM GRATEFUL FOR

....

....

....

....

ONE THING TO BE PROUD OF MYSELF FOR

....

....

....

....

Your Journal

The remainder of this book is designed to help you continue your journaling, and support you as you continue to explore your ADHD.

Each entry invites you to record an achievement, and then to consolidate everything you've done with a 30-day check-in and list of your key accomplishments.

There are 90 days' worth of journaling entries here, enough for you to establish a habit. However, I invite you to continue with a new journal when the time comes.

Make journaling a focal point of your day, and it will bring you so many rewards, becoming a huge part of your journey towards genuinely thriving with ADHD.

Day 1

Today's achievement:

Day 2

Today's achievement:

Day 3

....

....

....

....

....

....

....

....

....

Today's achievement:

....

Day 4

....

....

....

....

....

....

....

....

....

Today's achievement:

....

Day 5

....

....

....

....

....

....

....

....

....

Today's achievement:

....

Day 6

....

....

....

....

....

....

....

....

....

Today's achievement:

....

Day 7

....

....

....

....

....

....

....

....

Today's achievement:

....

Day 8

....

....

....

....

....

....

....

....

Today's achievement:

....

Day 9

....
....
....
....
....
....
....

Today's achievement:

....

Day 10

....
....
....
....
....
....
....

Today's achievement:

....

Day 11

....

....

....

....

....

....

....

....

....

....

Today's achievement:

....

Day 12

....

....

....

....

....

....

....

....

....

....

Today's achievement:

....

Day 13

Today's achievement:

Day 14

Today's achievement:

Day 15

....

....

....

....

....

....

....

....

....

Today's achievement:

....

Day 16

....

....

....

....

....

....

....

....

....

Today's achievement:

....

Day 17

....

....

....

....

....

....

....

....

....

Today's achievement:

....

Day 18

....

....

....

....

....

....

....

....

Today's achievement:

....

Day 19

....

....

....

....

....

....

....

....

....

Today's achievement:

....

Day 20

....

....

....

....

....

....

....

....

Today's achievement:

....

Day 21

....

....

....

....

....

....

....

....

....

....

Today's achievement:

....

Day 22

....

....

....

....

....

....

....

....

....

....

Today's achievement:

....

Day 23

....

....

....

....

....

....

....

....

....

Today's achievement:

....

Day 24

....

....

....

....

....

....

....

....

....

Today's achievement:

....

Day 25

Today's achievement:

Day 26

Today's achievement:

Day 27

....
....
....
....
....
....
....
....

Today's achievement:

....

Day 28

....
....
....
....
....
....
....
....

Today's achievement:

....

Day 29

....

....

....

....

....

....

....

....

Today's achievement:

....

Day 30

....

....

....

....

....

....

....

....

My key achievements this month:

....

....

Day 31

....

....

....

....

....

....

....

....

....

Today's achievement:

....

Day 32

....

....

....

....

....

....

....

....

....

Today's achievement:

....

Day 33

....

....

....

....

....

....

....

....

....

....

Today's achievement:

....

Day 34

....

....

....

....

....

....

....

....

....

....

Today's achievement:

....

Day 35

....

....

....

....

....

....

....

....

....

Today's achievement:

....

Day 36

....

....

....

....

....

....

....

....

....

Today's achievement:

....

Day 37

Today's achievement:

Day 38

Today's achievement:

Day 39

....

....

....

....

....

....

....

....

....

Today's achievement:

....

Day 40

....

....

....

....

....

....

....

....

....

Today's achievement:

....

Day 41

....

....

....

....

....

....

....

....

Today's achievement:

....

Day 42

....

....

....

....

....

....

....

....

Today's achievement:

....

Day 43

....

....

....

....

....

....

....

....

....

Today's achievement:

....

Day 44

....

....

....

....

....

....

....

....

....

Today's achievement:

....

Day 45

....
....
....
....
....
....
....
....

Today's achievement:

....

Day 46

....
....
....
....
....
....
....
....

Today's achievement:

....

Day 47

Today's achievement:

Day 48

Today's achievement:

Day 49

....

....

....

....

....

....

....

....

....

Today's achievement:

....

Day 50

....

....

....

....

....

....

....

....

Today's achievement:

....

Day 51

....
....
....
....
....
....
....
....

Today's achievement:

....

Day 52

....
....
....
....
....
....
....
....

Today's achievement:

....

Day 53

....

....

....

....

....

....

....

....

....

....

Today's achievement:

....

Day 54

....

....

....

....

....

....

....

....

....

Today's achievement:

....

Day 55

....

....

....

....

....

....

....

....

....

Today's achievement:

....

Day 56

....

....

....

....

....

....

....

....

....

Today's achievement:

....

Day 57

....

....

....

....

....

....

....

....

Today's achievement:

....

Day 58

....

....

....

....

....

....

....

....

Today's achievement:

....

Day 59

....

....

....

....

....

....

....

....

Today's achievement:

....

Day 60

....

....

....

....

....

....

....

....

My key achievements this month:

....

....

Day 61

....
....
....
....
....
....
....
....
....

Today's achievement:

....

Day 62

....
....
....
....
....
....
....
....
....

Today's achievement:

....

Day 63

_____

_____

_____

_____

_____

_____

_____

_____

_____

_____

Today's achievement:

_____

Day 64

_____

_____

_____

_____

_____

_____

_____

_____

_____

_____

Today's achievement:

_____

Day 65

Today's achievement:

Day 66

Today's achievement:

Day 67

Today's achievement:

Day 68

Today's achievement:

Day 69

....

....

....

....

....

....

....

....

Today's achievement:

....

Day 70

....

....

....

....

....

....

....

....

Today's achievement:

....

Day 71

....

....

....

....

....

....

....

....

....

Today's achievement:

....

Day 72

....

....

....

....

....

....

....

....

....

Today's achievement:

....

Day 73

Today's achievement:

Day 74

Today's achievement:

Day 75

....

....

....

....

....

....

....

....

Today's achievement:

....

Day 76

....

....

....

....

....

....

....

....

Today's achievement:

....

Day 77

Today's achievement:

Day 78

Today's achievement:

Day 79

Today's achievement:

Day 80

Today's achievement:

Day 81

Today's achievement:

Day 82

Today's achievement:

Day 83

Today's achievement:

Day 84

Today's achievement:

Day 85

....

....

....

....

....

....

....

....

....

....

Today's achievement:

....

Day 86

....

....

....

....

....

....

....

....

....

Today's achievement:

....

Day 87

Today's achievement:

Day 88

Today's achievement:

Day 89

....

....

....

....

....

....

....

....

Today's achievement:

....

Day 90

....

....

....

....

....

....

....

....

My key achievements this month:

....

....